I0140755

Imagine...
The Possabilities

Libbi Chilia

Halo
PUBLISHING
INTERNATIONAL

Dictionary definitions at the end of the book are from www.dictionary.com

1st Annual NubAbility Music City Camp in Nashville, TN. Photo courtesy of the NubAbility Athletics Foundation | Photographer: Andrew Harless (Page 26)

ISBN: 978-1-61244-684-4
Library of Congress Control Number: 2018960403

Printed in the United States of America

Halo Publishing International
1100 NW Loop 410
Suite 700 - 176
San Antonio, Texas 78213
1-877-705-9647
www.halopublishing.com
contact@halopublishing.com

This book is dedicated to Sami and Shelby who lovingly persuaded me to write another book. These two are not done showing the world just how amazing they are!
I love you, girls!

A special thank you to my husband, Tony, for his support and encouragement. Also, a heartfelt thank you to the young people who shared their stories with me:
Without your voice, I would have no book.

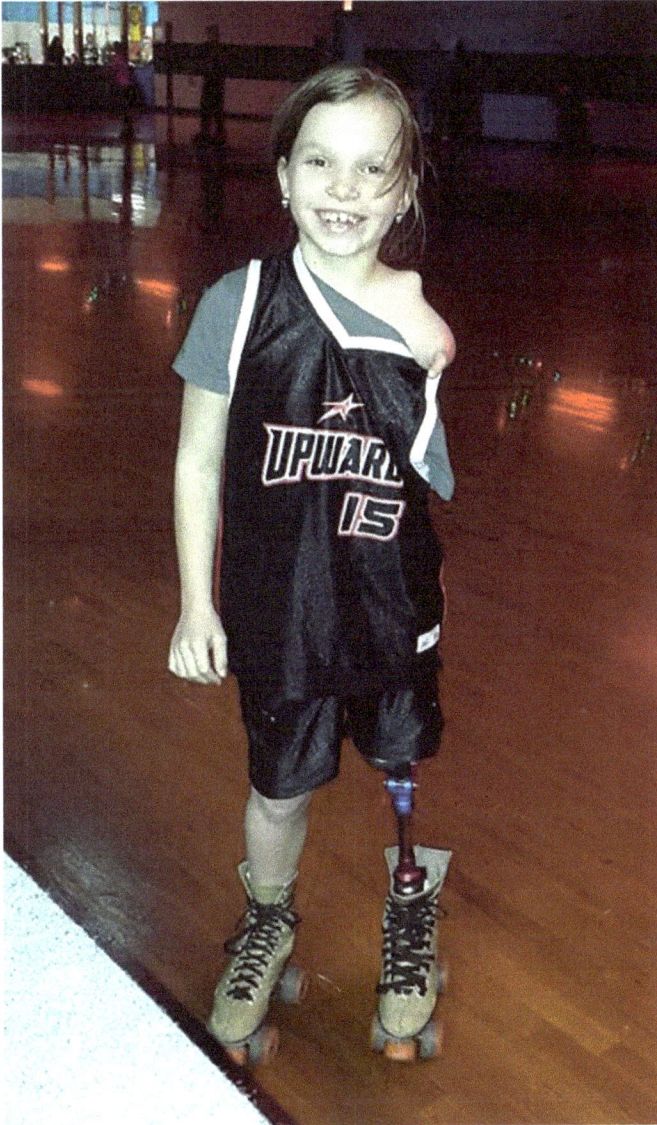

Brooklyn, 12, Michigan

Shayanne, 11, Ontario

I wonder what people see when they're looking at me. I wonder if they see what's there, or if they are focused on what is not. Do you see my passion and see that I won't be held back? Do you imagine all the possabilities in store for me?

Shelby, 13, Ohio

See Shelby's passion when she dances. Her grace and beauty inspire those who watch her perform. Shelby, age twelve, says that she conquers obstacles and learns how to do what she loves. "It may be different," asserts Shelby, "but I won't let anything stop me!" Shelby's inner strength allows her to push herself to achieve her goals and share her passion.

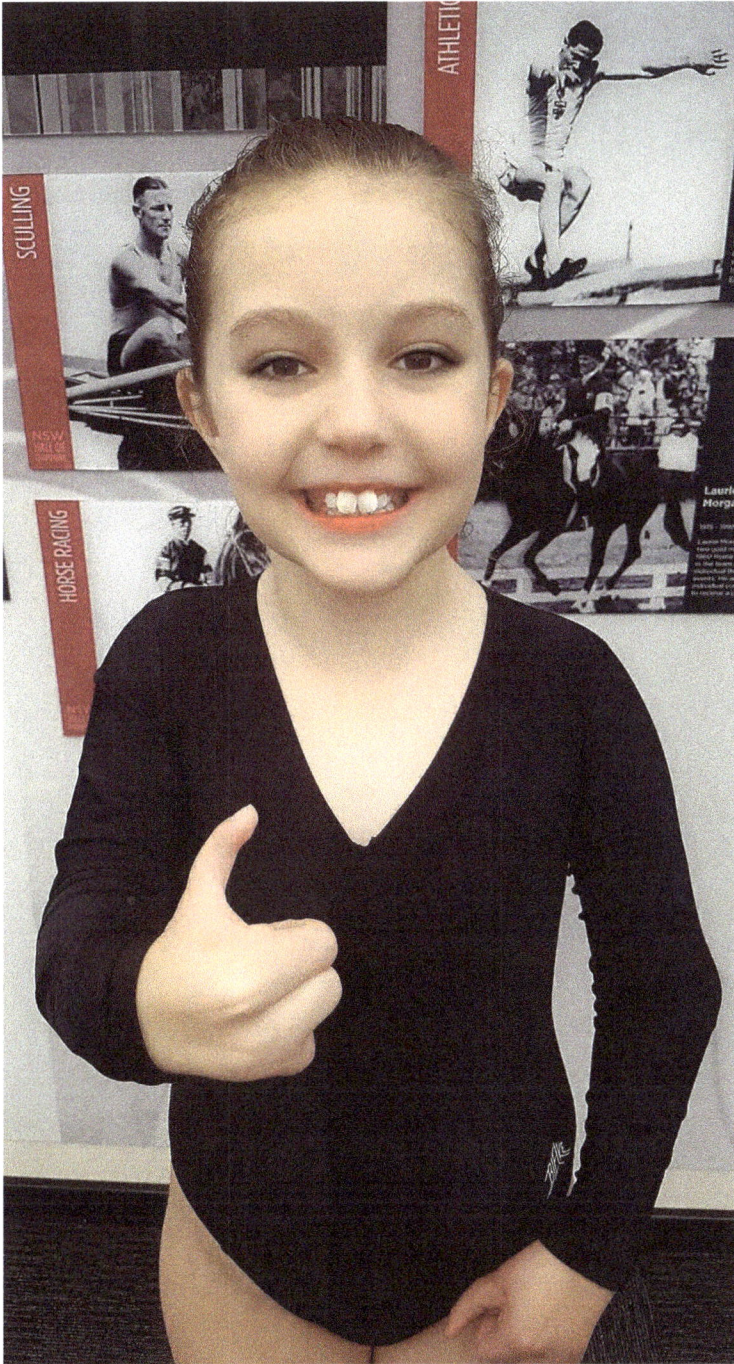

Sienna, age nine, develops her confidence through dance, and she recently added modeling and acting to her activities. Sienna shares videos with the world on YouTube to inspire others to do what they love. "Whether it's dancing, acting or modeling," Sienna says, "it not only makes my family proud but has my confidence soaring!" Diversity is positive, and our differences should be celebrated!

Sienna, 9, Australia

Bryant, 13, Georgia

See Bryant's drive when he shoots. Bryant, age thirteen, has been playing basketball since he was seven. He admits that it can be difficult, but his determination and practice landed Bryant a spot on his school's basketball team. In one game, Bryant scored thirteen points with nine rebounds! Bryant says that he will play basketball for as long as he can, and he's glad others are inspired by his drive to do his best!

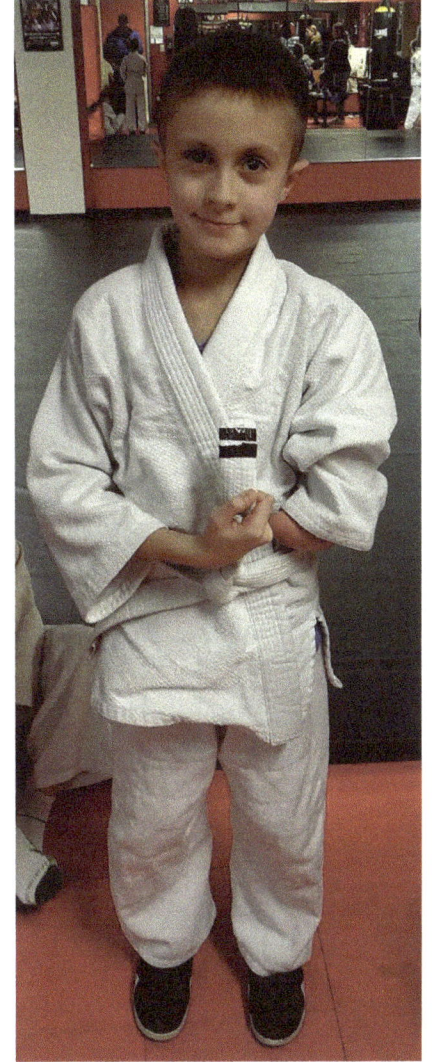

Brandon, 12, Indiana

"Having a limb difference challenges me to be a stronger person," says Brandon. He explains, "Some people think having one arm prevents me from doing things, but I prove that I can do anything when I make up my mind." Whether it's on the baseball field or at a Jiu-Jitsu tournament, Brandon adapts to join in and compete!

Brooklyn, 12, Michigan

Imagine all the poss*abilities*! Do you see what I see? Passion and drive to compete and achieve! Strength comes from within, so there's no reason to set limits.

Jack, 9, South Dakota

See Jack's focus as he practices sparring techniques. Taekwondo builds mental strength and focus, which Jack uses when he challenges an opponent or tests for a new belt. Jack shares, "Kicks are harder for me because I can't feel one foot and balance, but I adapt." He says he is encouraged by his instructors and parents, and he knows that he inspires others by learning different ways to do everything all the other kids are doing.

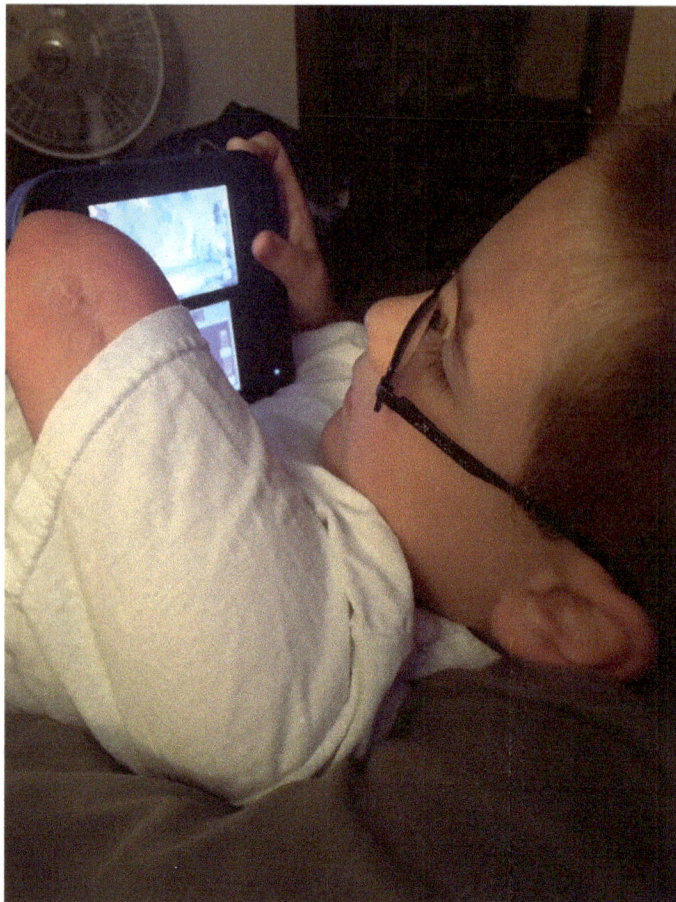

Devin, 9, Ohio

See Devin's determination to take on new challenges. Nine-year-old Devin wants to enjoy the same activities as everyone else. His friends play video games, so he worked really hard to figure out how to use the controllers.

"It was challenging to learn with only one arm," admits Devin. However, Devin wouldn't give up. Now, Devin can use the controllers on all the systems, and he has fun with his friends. Imagine Devin, stronger with one arm than many with two.

Julia, 11, Ohio

See Julia's strength as she rides horses. Julia says that she feels stronger being able to do with one leg what others do with two. Her inner strength feeds her physical strength as she finds her passion for riding horses. "Sometimes when I ride my horse, I think I could ride better if I had another leg just like the other girls," Julia admits. "Then I stop and think, wait a minute, I'm perfectly fine the way I am, and I can ride just as well with one leg; maybe even better than most people can with two legs!"

Hannah, 10, Iowa

Perseverance keeps ten-year-old Hanna's goals in sight. Having lower-limb difference makes running a challenge, but competition pushes her to work toward her goals. Hanna says, "I had a hard time keeping up with my sisters at first. I kept running every day so that I could be in a race with them." Finding ways to adapt and learn to do something challenging makes crossing the finish line even sweeter.

Brooklyn, 12, Michigan

Imagine all the poss*abilities*! Do you see what I see? Focus, determination, and strength to reach their goals, inspiring others along the way! With a will to achieve, obstacles will be overcome to prove to others, and myself, that perseverance means the most.

BJ, 18, Virginia

See BJ's grit as he rides the waves! BJ, age eighteen, admits that having upper and lower limb differences forced him to go out of his comfort zone and try everything to prove to others that he can do anything when he sets his mind to the task. "Growing up with a limb difference has made me a stronger person because oftentimes other people will automatically assume that I can't do something because I was born differently." BJ shows everyone just what he can do by playing wheelchair basketball, sled hockey, and, of course, surfing!

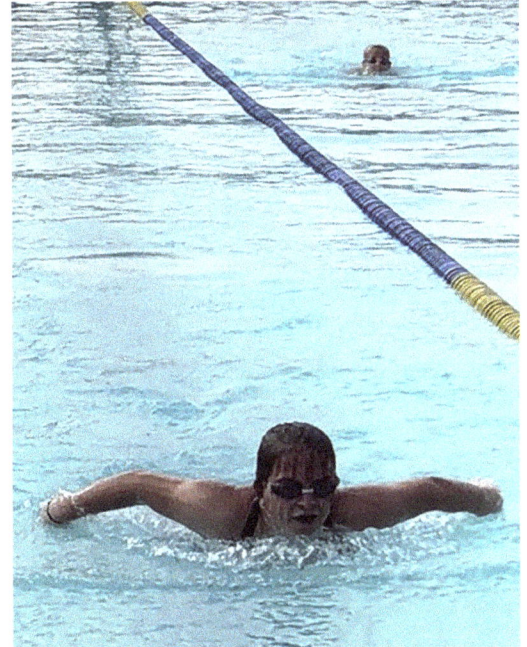

Sami, 14, Ohio

See Sami's tenacity as she glides through the water. Knowing that the only limitations that she has are the ones she puts on herself, fourteen-year-old Sami strives to develop her skills. Sami enjoys a challenge, especially when it comes to swimming. "When somebody doesn't believe I can swim, I say, "Race me!" Then, I win!"

See Hayden's spirit as she cheers on her team! Eleven-year-old Hayden has proved to fans that she is sure to find a way to cheer her team to victory! Hayden says that she knows that people are inspired when they see her cheer. She also admits that some moves are more difficult for her because of her limb difference. However, Hayden says, "I never say I can't. I just say that I might do it differently."

Hayden, 11, Washington

Shayanne, 11, Ontario

Shayann is persistent as he learns musical instruments. Shayann, age eleven, loves to learn musical instruments. Almost being rejected before he was given a chance to try, Shayann advocated for himself by saying to the instructors, "Show me what to do. I will figure out for myself how I will do it." Once they saw his optimism, he was accepted and learned to play guitar, piano and the harmonica!

Ava, 10, Missouri

Challenges help us to learn new things and allow our brains to grow. Learning to ride a bike was challenging for ten-year-old Ava. Her tenacity in learning the skill is one of her shining moments. "It was hard for me to get my balance because of my little arm. I kept trying and eventually managed to discover what worked best for me! This made me proud and really happy!"

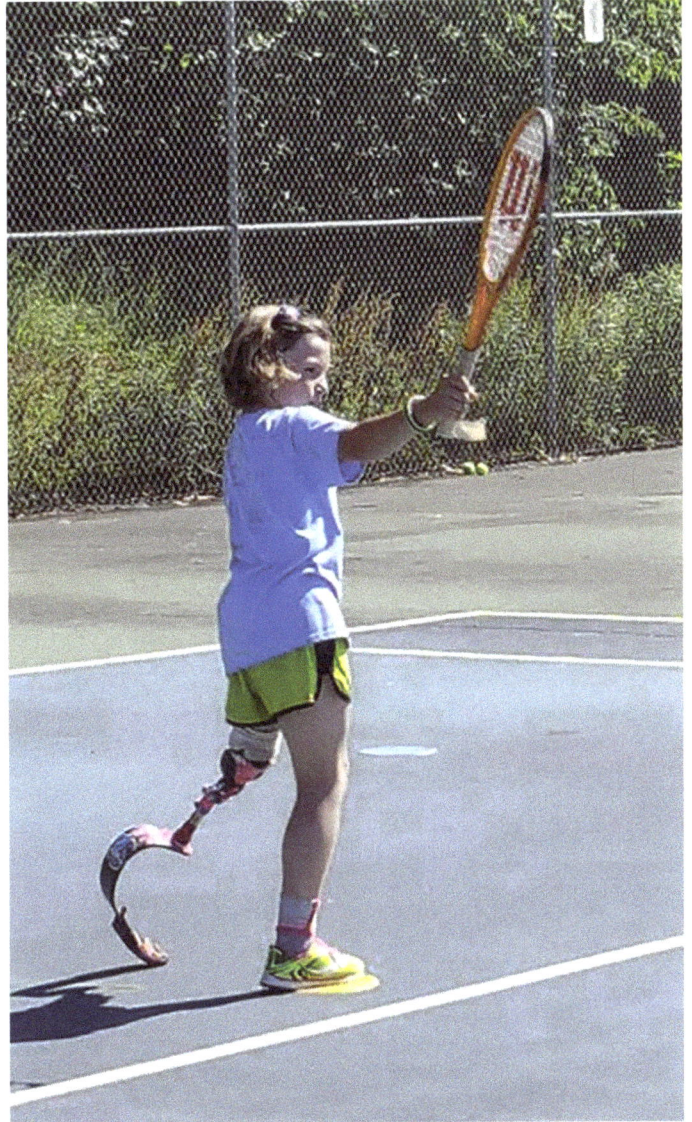

Zyra, 16, & Brooklyn, 12, Michigan

Brooklyn, 12, Michigan

Imagine all the poss*abilities*! Do you see what I see? Grit, tenacity, and spirit to show the world they are unstoppable! It's not always easy to reach the next level or learn a new skill. Believe in yourself to prove to yourself that your goals are worth the struggle.

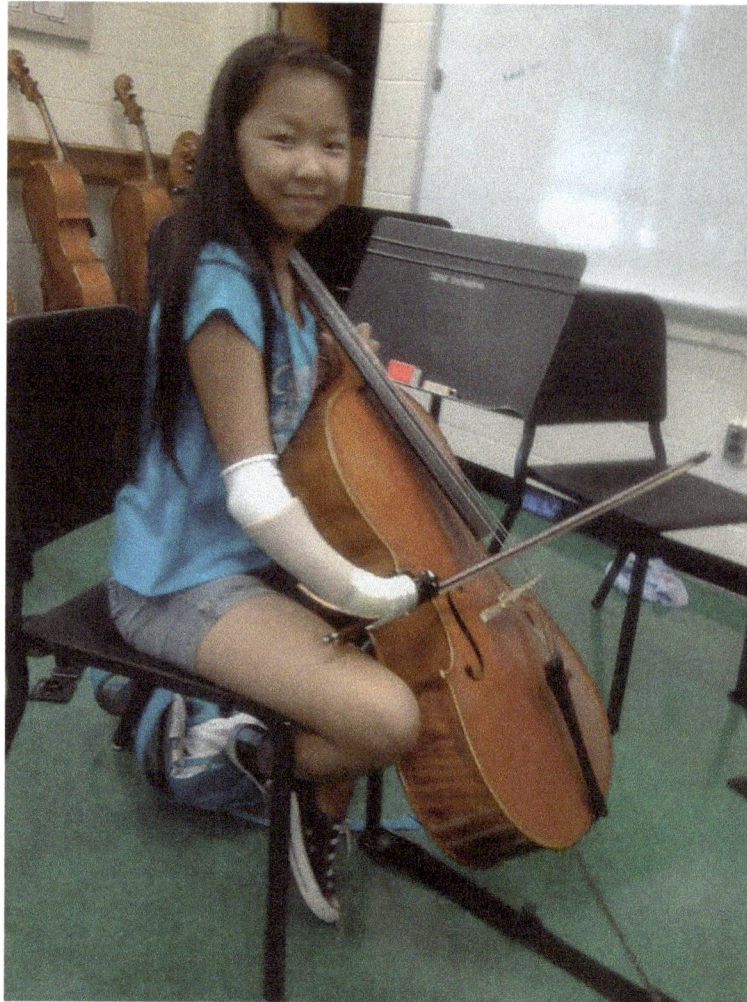

Lally, 17, California

See Lally's fervor as she plays the cello. Lally, age seventeen, learned to draw positive attention to her missing hand. "I realized that there was no way I could make myself unseen, so I decided to manipulate the way I was viewed. Instead of being quiet and trying to deny what was wrong with me, I forced myself to be outgoing and loud to draw attention to myself." People are going to stare, so Lally took control over what they would see.

Heidi, 14, Kansas

See Heidi's pride in gymnastics. Heidi, age fourteen, explains, "This picture shows a two-high, which is not the most difficult move I've done in gymnastics. My pride does not come from being able to hold my teammate up. My pride comes from my coach recognizing me as a strong, steady base. By choosing me as the base, he showed that he didn't see me as weak and delicate, but as someone he could count on to be strong." Heidi understands that she is going to draw attention, and she hopes that attention is for what she's able to control: her strength and endurance.

See Zayne's glee as he fishes. Zayne, age seven, describes his hands as "lucky fins." He is aware that people watch him as he reels in the catch of the day by himself, and he likes to use the moment to show spectators that there isn't anything that he can't do. Zayne has been known to motivate his friends by telling them, "If I can do it, so can you!"

Zayne, 8, Alabama

Camping has made great memories for Olivia. Hiking and archery have allowed thirteen-year-old Olivia to enjoy time with friends and family. Olivia shares, "From having to go through surgeries and physical therapy, I've overcome many challenges, which has made me a stronger person." Camping allows time for fun and relaxation, especially when sitting by the fire.

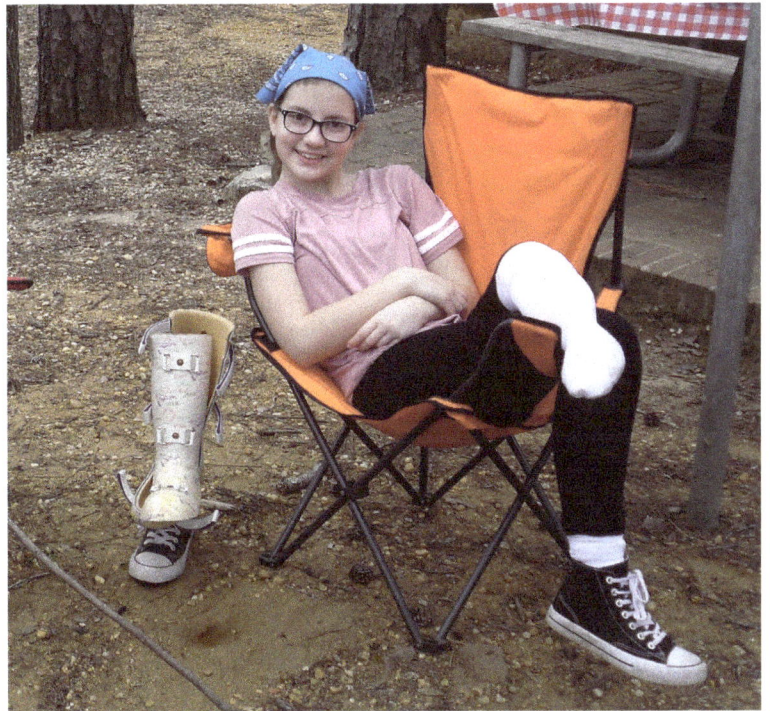

Olivia, 13, New Jersey

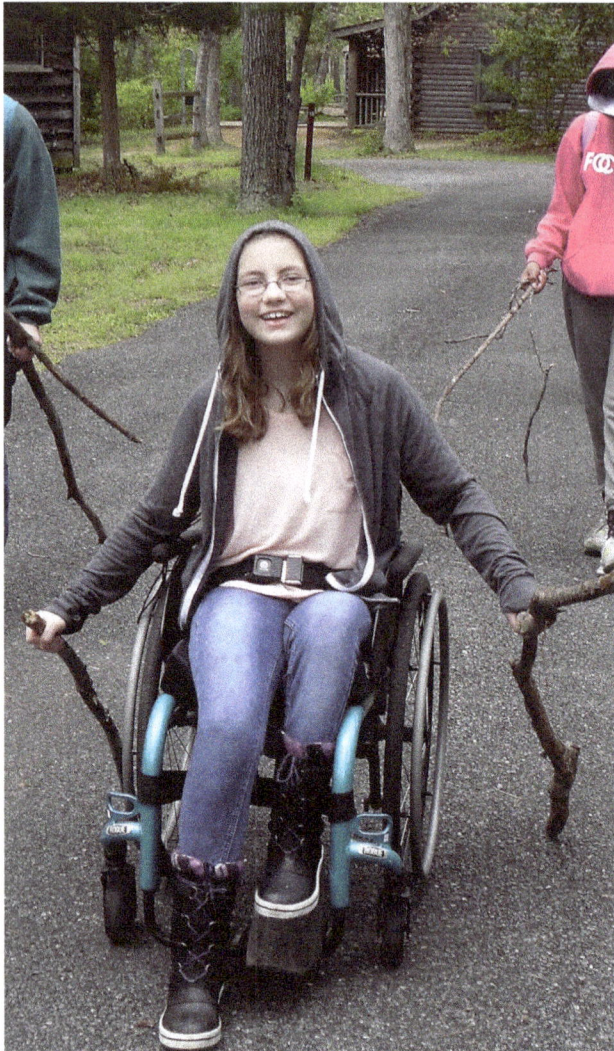

Olivia, 13, New Jersey

Sabrina, 23, Tennessee &
Brooklyn, 12, Michigan

People cannot be measured only by the length of their limbs. Instead, a person is measured by their passion, perseverance, grit, and tenacity. Take time to look, not at what is missing, but by what is there. To all people who stop and see, you'll be able to imagine all the poss*abilities*.

Vocabulary

Amputation — To surgically remove

Bilateral — Affecting both sides

Congenital — A disease or condition that is presented at birth

Extremity — Outermost part of body: hand, foot

Limb — Arm or leg

Prosthesis — An artificial body part

Unilateral — Affecting one side

Support and Information

Amputee Blade Runners (amputeebladerunners.com)

International Adoption Net (internationaladoptionnet.org)

International Child Amputee Network (I-CAN) (Child-amputee.net)

Mary Free Bed Rehabilitation Hospital (www.maryfreebed.com)

NubAbility Athletics (www.nubability.org)

PFFD (Proximal Femoral Focal Deficiency)/CFD(Congenital Femoral Deficiency)

Shriners Hospitals for Children (shrinershospitalsforchildren.org)